The Art
of Teaching

Words of Thanks
and Encouragement
for Teachers

ISBN: 0-7407-1912-2

Library of Congress Catalog Card Number: 2001086428

www.vickyhoward.com

The Art
of Teaching

Words of Thanks
and Encouragement
for Teachers

Illustrated by Vicky Howard
Edited by Pat Regan

**Andrews McMeel
Publishing**

Kansas City

The art of teaching is the art of assisting discovery.

—Pablo Casales

Has there ever been a profession that was at the same time so underappreciated yet so rewarding, so frustrating and so utterly fulfilling, a profession where tiny steps and minor victories mean so very much to the lives of others?

Teaching is more than a job, more than a profession. It is a vocation, a calling to open young minds (and sometimes not-so-young minds) to the wonders and possibilities of the world in which we live. The best teachers know that education is a lifelong journey and that teaching a child to *want* to learn is more important than any single lesson.

If you've seen the face of a sixth-grade teacher who's managed to keep control of her class the entire week before Christmas vacation, you've gazed into the eyes of a hero. We must never underestimate the strength of character and the sheer will that is required of teachers. In the end, there's not just one reason—or even a handful of reasons—why they answer the call of the schoolbell every day. There are hundreds of reasons, and each has a first name.

In this book, illustrator Vicky Howard pays tribute through her art to her own teachers and to teachers everywhere—those multifaceted persons who are equal parts scholar, entertainer, coach, parent, counselor, and confidant. All of our lives have in some way been touched by a teacher, and for this we should be truly grateful.

Teachers
open the door,
but you must
enter by yourself.

Chinese proverb

An investment in
knowledge
always pays the
best dividends.

Benjamin Franklin

plant the seeds of knowledge.

Reach for the
high apples first;
you can get the
low ones anytime.

Proverb

Nothing great was
ever achieved
without enthusiasm.

Ralph Waldo Emerson

Education is not
preparation for life;
education is life itself.

John Dewey

September days
are glad days,
for school has now begun,
We'll have to work
and study hard,
But also we'll have fun!

Maude Grant,
The Instructor, 1926

The greatest
masterpieces
were once only
pigments on a palette.

Henry S. Haskins

A joy that's shared
is a joy made double.

English proverb

AIM HIGH, TIME FLIES!

Choose a job you love,
and you will never
have to work a
day in your life.

Confucius

Make the best
of everything;
Think the best
of everything;
Hope the best
for yourself.

George Stephenson

Smile a little,
Help a little,
Push a little,
The world needs you.
Work a little,
Wait a little,
Hope a little,
And don't get blue.

E.O.G.

Teachers
open our eyes
and warm our
hearts.

There is nothing like putting the shine on another face to put the shine on your own.

Gannet

We learn by doing,
achieve by pursuing.

Teachers
encourage us
to let our
imaginations soar.

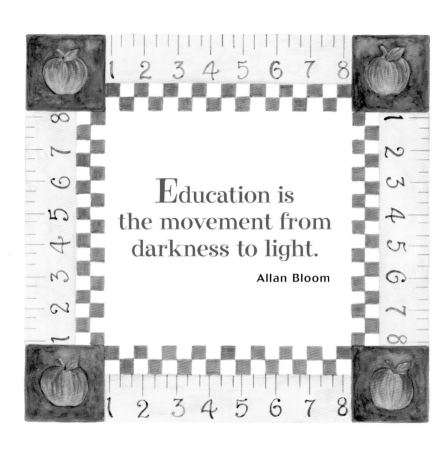

Education is
the movement from
darkness to light.

Allan Bloom

By learning
you will teach;
by teaching
you will learn.

Latin proverb

The brighter you are,
the more you
have to learn.

Don Herold

Teachers
are the
brightest
colors
in the
quilt
of life.

If you have the knowledge,
let others light their
candles by it.

Thomas Fuller

Education is ... hanging
around until you've
caught on.

Robert Frost

a b c
1 2 3
apple
BLUE
GREEN
RED
YELLOW
FIRST READER
MUSIC HOUR
Book 1

The fruits of teaching are harvested for a lifetime.

Lessons hard to learn
are sweet to know.

Proverb

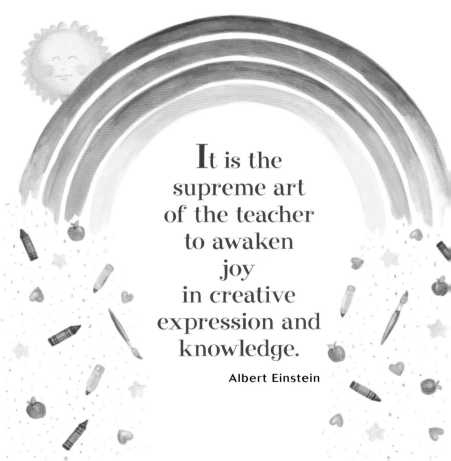

It is the
supreme art
of the teacher
to awaken
joy
in creative
expression and
knowledge.

Albert Einstein

Experience is a hard teacher because she gives the test first, the lesson afterward.

Vernon Law

Every road has
hills to be
climbed.

Happiness
lies in the joy
of achievement
and the thrill of
creative effort.

Franklin D. Roosevelt

To know how
to suggest is the
art of teaching.
Proverb

The mediocre teacher tells.
The good teacher explains.
The superior teacher demonstrates.
The great teacher inspires.

William Arthur Ward

All words are pegs
to hang ideas on.

Proverb

apple

crayon

a b c
1 2 3

PENCIL

1 2 3

art

SPELLING

BEE

BOOKS

Inspiration
comes of working
every day.

Baudelaire

Write on your heart
that every day
is the best day
of the year.

Ralph Waldo Emerson

The scenes of childhood
are the memories
of future years.

The Farmers' Almanac, 1850

The dog that ate the homework!

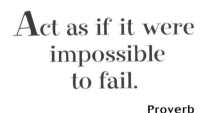

Act as if it were impossible to fail.

Proverb

Every day that
we spend without
learning something is
a day lost.

Beethoven

Learning is a treasure that will follow its owner everywhere.

Chinese proverb

School
is a
scrapbook
of happy
memories.

You have to work
the life out of you
to keep the life in you.

Proverb

I've just found out—
Perhaps you knew it—
That work's just play
When you love to do it!

Alice E. Allen

The future
belongs to those
who believe
in the beauty
of their dreams.

Eleanor Roosevelt

Teaching
today
touches
tomorrow.

The best part of a book
is not the thought it contains
but the thought it suggests.

Proverb

Oh, how fine it is to know a thing or two!

Molière

The art
of teaching
is the art of
assisting
discovery.

Pablo Casales

Where your heart is,
there will your
treasure be also.

Proverb

The greatest gift is a portion of yourself.

Ralph Waldo Emerson

As the heart
makes the home,
the teacher
makes the child.

Proverb

The man who does not
read good books
has no advantage
over the man
who cannot read them.

Mark Twain

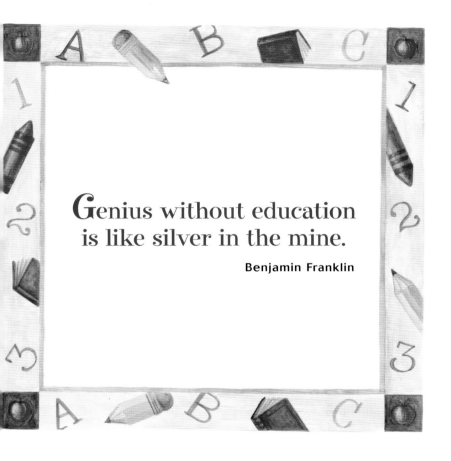

Genius without education
is like silver in the mine.

Benjamin Franklin

Imagination

s more important than knowledge.
Knowledge is limited.

Imagination encircles the world.

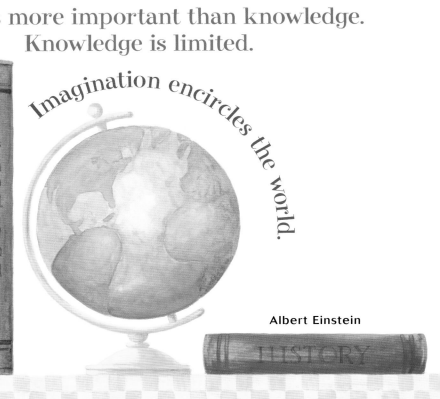

Albert Einstein

God grant me the serenity
to accept the things
I cannot change,
courage to change
the things I can,
and wisdom to
know the difference.

When you come to
the end of your rope,
tie a knot and hang on.

Franklin D. Roosevelt

*Life is not a cup
to be drained
but a measure
to be filled.*

Proverb

Along with success
comes a reputation
for wisdom.

Euripides

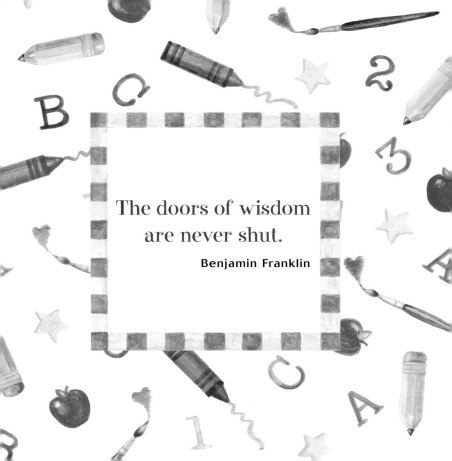

The doors of wisdom
are never shut.

Benjamin Franklin

My heart is singing
for the joy of this morning.
A miracle has happened!
The light of understanding
has shown upon my pupil's mind,
and behold, all things are changed!

Annie Sullivan

Bless
our
Teachers

Education
is simply the
soul of a
society as it
passes from one
generation
to another.

G. K. Chesterton

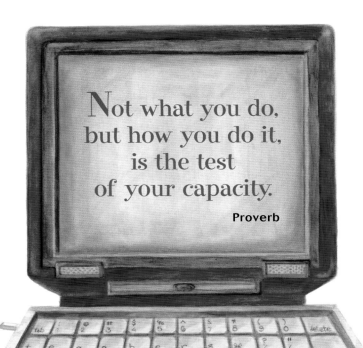

Not what you do,
but how you do it,
is the test
of your capacity.

Proverb

It's not the load
but the way
you carry it.

Proverb

Happiness adds and multiplies as we divide it with others.

Proverb

To teach is to
learn twice.

Joseph Joubert

They can, because they
believe they can.

Virgil

A book is
like a garden
carried in the pocket.

Proverb

Words are the flowers
in our language garden.

Proverb

$\mathbf{A}$ teacher makes a point in man

ifferent ways.

Books are the windows
through which we
see the world.

Proverb

Children
are our most
valuable resource.

Herbert Hoover

He who can reach
a child's heart
can reach the
world's heart.

Rudyard Kipling

Teachers
hold the key
to a bright
future.

Happy are
they who have
wisdom—and
may you
be the
happiest of all.

Proverb

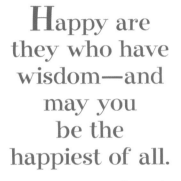